CW00726515

Learning to Pray

Copyright © 1995 CPAS
First edition 1995. All rights reserved

Published by **CPAS**, Athena Drive, Tachbrook Park, WARWICK CV34 6NG.

ISBN 1 8976 6051 0
British Library Cataloguing-in-Publication Data.
A catalogue record for this book is available from the British Library.

Cover design by Phil Gill• Design by Catherine Jackson
Printed by Unigraph Printing Services

Church Pastoral Aid Society • Registered Charity No 1007820
A company limited by guarantee

INTRODUCTION

'For those who truly desire a life of prayer, the only way to achieve it is by praying.'

Mother Mary Clare SLG

'To pray is to stand spiritually before God in our heart in glorification, thanksgiving, supplication and contrite penitence.'
Theophilus the Recluse

Many of us would agree with this wonderful statement about prayer. But in the next breath we say: 'I can't do it.' What's going on? Which of the following excuses do you ever make?

♦ I'm too bad to pray.
♦ God doesn't really like me, even if he loves me.
♦ I can't pray like it's taught in the books.
♦ I'm a person of action; I let other people do the praying.
♦ When I pray it doesn't make any difference.
♦ I haven't got time.

In an age which has spawned the cult of the expert and which idolizes independence it can be hard to accept Jesus' recommendation that we enter the Kingdom as little children. As children we will naturally totter and fall and walk again. The truth is that we grow into maturity by becoming increasingly *more* dependent on a Father who picks up and carries, shares our tears and delights, forgives and urges, and dearly wants us to talk to him. He longs for us to ask questions, express our pleasures and bewilderments, admit anger and jealousies, and expose our dreams. And it can be just as important to enjoy being with someone without having to talk. In God's company there can be a silence of awe as well as of intimacy.

Prayer can be expressed in as many ways as there are people. What matters is that our hearts and minds are open to God. Children (and often mentally disabled people) are naturally trusting and frank. But adults have to learn and develop an inner awareness of a God who is there, whose presence is already with us.

Prayer gets 'stuck' when we block off certain areas of ourselves which we are afraid to face. So we make progress in prayer when we are able to include the 'sticking point' and proceed in the light of deeper understanding and experience.

♦ Have you ever given up on prayer? What was going on then?
♦ What do you find hard about prayer?

Prolonged periods of dryness, darkness, uncertainly or disappointment can force our roots to reach for unexpected sources of nourishment when we discover the diverse ways in which God communicates with us. Sometimes refreshment comes from drinking in from different Christian traditions. This book offers just such an opportunity.

Using this book

This is a practical workbook designed for use in small groups, but it may also be used by individuals. In it we have tried to introduce Christians to various forms of prayer, just giving a taste of each to whet the appetite.

Each chapter begins with THINKING THROUGH which offers background information and guidance. One or two pages of GROUP FOCUS give a selection of practical activities to help group members get involved in each form of prayer and experience for themselves the style and feel of each one. The TALKING POINTS section offers opportunity to look at Scripture and gives further resources for discussion. As this book is designed for use in small groups, the pages may be photocopied.

The authors

Pat Heritage works alongside her husband Barry in parish ministry in York. She is involved with the Acorn Christian Healing Trust as a tutor. She has experience of leading workshops and 'Away Days' for CPAS.

Jenny Hellyer was a teacher and musician before living and working in the Lee Abbey Community. She lives in Nottingham with husband Steve, a clergyman, and their two young children. She's now a full-time mum with occasional forays into ministry and music.

Liz Culling is priest-in-charge of St Michael's, Cherry Burton in the East Riding of Yorkshire. She is also an adviser to the diocese on rural ministry. Prior to this Dr Culling taught church history and spirituality at Cranmer Hall in Durham.

Annie Hughes is married to John who is a vicar in Birmingham. Together they have led church weekends and retreats.

Gill Bewley, a trained teacher, worked alongside her late husband Graham in parishes in London, Hull, Sheffield and Rotherham. As a CPAS regional assistant, she helps in setting up Ministry among Women events in South Yorkshire. She is active in her own local parish in Sheffield where she is a Reader.

Debbie Seddon is married to Philip and has three children. She teaches part-time but primarily likes being at home.

Meditation

As I write continual rain has been falling, bringing to an end a long spell of hot, dry weather. Fortunately the rain is light and has had time slowly but surely to penetrate the rock-hard surface of the flower-borders. As it soaks further down it will eventually reach the roots of the plants, bringing renewed life. Had the rain fallen too heavily it would have run straight off the borders, without benefit to the flowers.

The rain reminds me that meditation is about slowing down so as to enable God's Word not just to pass over the surface of my mind but to penetrate through and soak into my whole being. It renews my mind, changes my heart and affects my attitudes, actions and relationships, both with God and other people.

Meditation on God's Word can also be likened to chewing food which, when digested, becomes part of me: 'When your words came, I ate them; they were my joy and my heart's delight, for I bear your name, O Lord God Almighty.' (Jeremiah 15:16)

What happens when I meditate?

I slow down opening my mind and heart to God.

I tell God about my desires, concerns and needs.

I read and re-read a short passage of Scripture. I read it slowly and leisurely, not analytically, letting the words sink in. I expect God to speak to me in a personal way so that his Word becomes alive, relevant and applicable to me for today, in my present circumstances. I use only the Bible. This differs from Bible study where the emphasis is more on learning *about* Scripture with the help of commentaries and notes in order to gain important intellectual understanding.

I reflect and ponder, asking the Holy Spirit to help me discover and listen to what God is saying to me, slowly 'chewing' over the words, giving myself time to 'digest' them. I ask myself: 'What am I to know; to believe; to be; to do?' Sometimes I substitute my name in appropriate places – for example, instead of 'Israel' in Hosea 11:1-4. Or I will use 'I' or 'me', in place of 'they' or 'them' in Psalm 106.

I respond to God. Personal response is another side of the two-way communication we call prayer.

I talk (sometimes aloud) to him about what he is saying to me through his Word. I may want to thank him; say sorry; ask for his help for other people or difficult situations in his church and his world. I may just want to sit with him; worship him; say, 'I love you'. As I talk I continue to listen to anything else he may want to say to me.

I make decisions about the way I live this day in my life, resulting from anything he has shown me.

I receive fully whatever God has said, letting his word 'dwell in my heart' (Colossians 3:16-17). I remain quiet before him; thanking him; maybe opening my hands symbolically to demonstrate my acceptance of his Word. I don't rush away but wait in his presence, continuing to listen for anything further God wants to say.

I remember what God has said by recording it in ways which will help me continue meditating. A verse (or word)

of Scripture can be memorized or written on a small card and placed where I can see it – for example, on my desk, by the telephone, on the fridge door. Three-dimensional reminders – a stone, a shell, a pin-figure drawing or symbol – can be useful when I only have a short time in which to meditate. Recording in a notebook helps me see what God has been saying over a period of time – for, as with digestion, the results are not always immediately obvious!

Being filled

It is important to realize that Christian meditation differs fundamentally from meditation as practised in religions of the East (for example, transcendental meditation), where the aim is to empty one's mind so as to arrive at a thought-free state.

In Christian meditation the aim is to have one's mind and heart filled with the Word of God so that we may have an encounter with him in which a two-way communication takes place. We listen as God shares the thoughts of his mind and the desires of his heart, bringing us understanding, guidance and nourishment (Isaiah 55). God listens as we share with him our

thoughts, desires and needs (Matthew 7:7-8) and offer him our worship, adoration and thanksgiving.

God longs for that encounter. He invites us to come to meet with him (James 4:8), to know him personally – not just facts about him (Psalm 46:10), and to receive from him (Isaiah 55).

This is not achieved by self-effort and striving, but by being still before him (Psalm 46:10), confident that we have access to him through Jesus (Ephesians 2:18). Increasingly the desire of our heart will be God himself – not for what he can do for us.

Joyful encounter

But when you pray, go into your room, close the door and pray to your Father, who is unseen. Then your Father, who sees what is done in secret, will reward you.
(Matthew 6:6)

Encountering God brings reward – not given grudgingly, but abundantly. The Greek word translated here as 'room' in fact means 'treasure chamber'. It is interesting to note that the 'room' has no exclusion notice! All disciples are able to enter whatever our temperament, situation, experience, background, age or lifestyle. We

need no particular expertise, calling, ministry or method to qualify us. The room has no detailed instructions as to where, and when to enter, how long to stay, or what approach to use!

It is important not to confuse guidelines suggested by others (as in this workbook!) with specific scriptural instruction. Such confusion can leave us feeling frustrated, inferior or angry. Jesus does not put such burdens on us. He wants us to experience, and be enriched by, his Father.

Therefore it is important to note carefully and respond to what Jesus *does* say here about encountering God in prayer. He speaks of three essentials:

♦ We need to spend some time with God. Jesus says *when*, not if we pray. We need space to slow down and be available to God.

♦ We need to find a 'store-room' – a place to be alone with God.

♦ We need to shut out distractions and interruptions.

Blessed is the man who does not walk in the counsel of the wicked or stand in the way of sinners or sit in the seat of mockers. But his delight is in the law of the Lord, and on his law he meditates day and night. He is like a tree planted by streams of water, which yields its fruit in season and whose leaf does not wither. Whatever he does prospers.

Psalm 1:1-3

Space in my life

'Jesus
punctuated his
life with silence
and solitude...
they gave the
rest of his life its
structure,
direction and
balance.'

David
Runcorn

Being practical

It is at this point that the 'essentials' can be defeated by the apparent 'impossibles' – and we are tempted to give up. But there is a way forward if we let go of how we think we should pray and ask ourselves:

♦ What is practically possible for me in my situation, with my temperament, at this present time in my life?

♦ When can I be available to God?
As I would with a friend. When can I arrange longer get-togethers, look for shorter chats, be alert for unexpected opportunities?
As I would in business. Make an appointment. Don't double book!

♦ Ask: Can I get up earlier? Can I give up something – a television programme, for example?

♦ Aim for 'quality time' rather than quantity of time.

Where can I be alone with God?

Your 'room' could be:

In a friend's house, the attic, a garden shed, the garage, church, the office (if not shared), the garden, the park, your route while dog-walking (you could listen to Scripture on a personal stereo), travelling to work on the bus, anywhere where you are able to close your eyes to your surroundings.

Making this space in your life may involve arranging for a baby-sitter. It may mean appraising how family responsibilities are shared.

How can I give my attention to God?

It won't be easy if, like Jesus, you lead a busy life, or if, like Peter, you have an 'activist' temperament.

♦ *Outwardly* Tell people when you are unavailable. Disconnect the phone. Use ear-plugs to muffle the sound of noisy neighbours or loud music. Find a comfortable, but alert, position in which to pray.

♦ *Inwardly* Switch off your mental 'inner tape' to concentrate on God by 'centring down'.

♦ *Physically* Be still. Relax each part of your body. Close your eyes. Slow down and deepen your breathing.

♦ Mentally 'Gather-up' your thoughts. Offer them to God. Release them into his care. Close the door on them.

'Centre' on God by listening to music, looking at a picture, or a particular symbol such as a cross, a lighted candle or a flower. Become aware of God's presence.

Use one of the names of God as a focus of 'worth-ship'. Claim a promise of God's nearness (James 4:8). Imagine yourself entering the audience chamber of the King of Kings (Revelation 4:9-11; 5:11-14; Isaiah 6:3). Picture yourself approaching him. Gaze on his greatness. Adore, sing or tell him you love him. Be trustfully quiet in our loving Father's presence, enjoying his company, available to him.

Heart's desire

Encountering God through meditation on his Word touches our emotions positively; it gives practical direction; through nourishing us, it resources others; and it produces fruit (Psalm 119; Isaiah 55:10-11, Luke 8:15). The key is our heart's desire (Psalm 119:2). Our starting point may be a prayer: 'Holy Spirit stir my heart.'

GROUP IDEAS

Slow reading

You may find it helpful to read the chosen passage aloud. Read and re-read it slowly, not analysing but 'savouring' it. Linger with any word or phrase that attracts your attention. Stay with it 'cherishing', 'chewing', 'digesting' it. This is God speaking to you now in your present situation. Respond either in silence, or by speaking out to God whatever is in your mind or on your heart. You may find you don't get past the first few words. After a while, or on another occasion, return to the passage and continue the process. End by talking to God, or being silent with him as you would with a close friend.

Suggested passages
Psalm 139:1-18; Isaiah 40: 9-31; Isaiah 55; Matthew 6:5-14; Matthew 8:23-27; Luke 14:1-14; Philippians 2:1-11.

GROUP IDEAS

Short meditations

Centre down.
Read the passage.

Ask:
♦ How do I feel?
♦ Did God say anything to me?
♦ Did anything important stand out?
♦ Were there any difficulties?
♦ Talk to God about your answers.

Suggested passages
Psalm 1:1-3; Isaiah 49:15-16; Isaiah 55:1-2; Matthew 6:33-34; Colossians 3:12-14; 1 John 4:9-10.

GROUP IDEAS

Dip into Psalm 119

♦ Read a few verses
♦ Record the feelings produced and discoveries made by the Psalmist as he meditates.
♦ Ponder using questions beginning How? What? Why? Whom? Where? Who?
♦ Ask God what he is saying to you about your meditation.

GROUP IDEAS

Unexpected opportunities
This activity should last about five minutes.

Wherever you are, enter your 'room'. Close your eyes if appropriate. Choose one of the following:

♦ Relax like a trusting child (Psalm 131:2).
♦ Enjoy being with God.
♦ Reflect on where you have seen God in your life today. Thank him.
♦ Focus on the single word 'Jesus', or one of the names of God – for example, 'Provider'.
♦ Remember God's truth: 'I am not alone' (Matthew 28:20); 'I am loved' (1 John 3:1).
♦ Use memory cards, a memorized verse, objects or nature as a visual reminder of God's word to you.
♦ Listen to worship, or Scripture on tape.
♦ Tell God how you are feeling. Ask him to show you his thoughts.
♦ When tired, allow words of a favourite hymn, perhaps 'How Great Thou Art', to speak for you.

*'God is not a good habit
a useful Sunday exercise
one interest
among others
a fascinating hobby*

*God is life itself
he is Someone
not to be
analysed
examined,
proved
but to be met*

*And when that happens
Life unfolds
meanings matter
love is deeper*

*Be still. Relax.
Unwind.
Open those inner doors.'*

Howard Booth

GROUP IDEAS

Throughout your day

Be alert to the Holy Spirit giving further insight into Scripture by looking around you at people, nature and everyday objects.

- *Nature*: Psalm 1:1-3; Matthew 6:26-30
- *Objects*: Jeremiah 18:1-6; Matthew 5:13
- *People*: Isaiah 49:15-16; Matthew 18:2-4; Luke 15:11-32
- *Jesus' statements about himself*: John 6:35; 8:12; 10:7; 11:25; 14:6; 15:5

GROUP IDEAS

Images of God

Write down a list of words or draw a picture of what God means to you. Compare your words or picture with what Jesus said about God in Luke's Gospel. Take one passage at a time.

Ask:
- What does each passage say about God?
- What is true in my thinking about God?
- What is false in my thinking about God?
- What is God saying to me?
- What do I want to say to God?

Suggested passages
Luke 6:35-36; 10:21-22; 11:11-13; 12:11-12; 22-32; 15:1-7; 15:11-32; 18:9-14; 20:38; 22:70; 24:46-49.

GROUP IDEAS

Sing a new song

Read one of the passages slowly.

- Consider the writer's experience of God.
- Allow the Holy Spirit to remind you of your own experience of God.
- Praise God for your experience of him in spoken or written word; or create a new song.

Suggested passages
1 Chronicles 16:8-36; 29:10-13; Psalm 8; Psalm 40:1-11; Psalm 103; Psalm 104; Ephesians 1:3-10; Revelation 15:3-4.

GROUP IDEAS

The words of Jesus

Imagine Jesus, by your side, speaking these words to you today.

Ask:
- How do they apply to me?
- What is Jesus saying to me?
- What changes is he asking me to make in my life?
- Talk to God about your answers.

Suggested passages
Matthew 5:13-14; 7:7-11; Mark 8:34-38; John 13:12-17; 14:1-4; 15:1-4.

Learning to Pray © CPAS 1995

Going further

Look at your week

	SUN	MON	TUES	WED	THU	FRI	SAT
A.M.							
P.M.							
Evening							

Where can I find time to be available for God?
How long is this?
Where can I find small spaces for God?
How long are these?
What could I do to make more space in my life for God?

Where can I be alone with God?
Name the place or places.
What help would I need to be alone?
Who could I ask to help me?
Could I offer a 'room' to someone else?

Summary
Decide My place of prayer will be ....
I will start on ....(day) at................ (time)
I will spend .... minutes with God.

Start with a short period of between ten and fifteen minutes.
    Centre down.
    Choose an exercise.
    Go slowly. If you don't finish the exercise you can continue on another occasion.
Be ready to learn: practise, persevere, expect the unexpected!
Be open, with no preconceived ideas.
Be eager to listen, receive and respond.
Find what works for you.
Discuss with others in your church what they have found helpful in prayer and meditation.
Talk over the possibility of going on a Quiet Day or a Day of Retreat – where someone will lead a meditation.
Read Luke Chapter 8:15.

YOUR COMMENTS

Creativity and Prayer

'He who sings prays twice.'

St Augustine

*A*ll prayer is creative. The Spirit of God breathed on the chaos that was the unformed universe, and life emerged.

That same Spirit – what a thought! – breathes through you and me as we pray. Again, life emerges as we say 'yes' to the privilege of being co-workers with him whose way is to bring glory to himself through men and women. The book of Acts is full of inspired prayer, where the power of God is released to heal the sick, open prison doors and bring salvation to thousands. Prayer brings adventure with God.

New horizons, one Lord

Through the centuries Christians have prayed in many different places, in many different cultures, in many different ways. We can learn from, and adopt, the many traditions surrounding us.

Sometimes traditions may grow stale. We and they may need renewing. In life we thrive on the stimulus of friendship, of holiday, of work or role, and of ministry to others. Prayer is about every part of life being caught up into God. And so it is healthy to allow him to continue to expand our horizons in prayer as in life, bringing the two together.

I lived in a Christian community for seven years. I am grateful for the many avenues of prayer which that experience opened for me. We came from many denominations and nations; our call to serve Jesus unified us, and his love enabled us to take the risk of accepting and exploring each other's ways of prayer.

More than words

Our western understanding leads us to assume that prayer is mostly verbal. But prayer can also involve gesture, music, pictures, and dance. The Holy Spirit gives a language of prayer (tongues) in which our own words are surrendered for his.

To begin to move into some of these areas is to find we can be helped to pray from a deeper place. We'll allow real feelings to emerge, and honest responses. God calls *all* of our being into fellowship with him.

We've also emphasized the mind. We need to pray with the mind but also with the Spirit (1 Corinthians 14:15). He is in the business of re-creating us as whole persons – the development of our imagination and senses is part of this restoring work.

Rediscovered joy

The Protestant tradition has tended to make prayer feel like work. Today the Holy Spirit is restoring the balance with a call to rediscover the importance in prayer of grace, of stillness, and of listening – with delightful consequences. I was recently praying for a little girl and found myself asking the question: 'What would Jesus do for her?' I was given a lovely picture in my imagination of her sitting happily on his knee. Her mother had been longing for such an expression of security for her daughter. She was encouraged by the vivid picture.

Words and actions

Jesus lived life to the full. He drew on all of life to teach the love of God. Lost coins, fig trees and sheep focus our understanding and capture the imagination. His actions spoke volumes: the water transformed into wine and a lame man healed tell us in real-life terms how good he is. So it's hardly surprising that he loves us to respond equally wholeheartedly to him. Whether in songs, or through praying for sick friends

or kneeling in adoration, he has given us all unique ways of expressing love for him.

Keeping a journal

Sometimes a verse of Scripture speaks to us with what seems like special significance. On another occasion a dream, for example, may seem particularly meaningful. Was it the Lord speaking? Committing these inklings to paper encourages us in faith, and helps us to learn to listen to God. Looking back, we see patterns unfolding. Keeping a journal can help us notice and appreciate God's involvement in our lives.

Praying in writing can help us to bring our true selves to God. We're often more honest while writing than when praying verbally. We don't always want to admit our emotional responses, but as we put pen to paper we give ourselves permission to do just that. Then we may well find God with us, in the midst of it – a healing exercise.

Prayer for lifestyle

Adapting to life's changing demands is a creative task. Sometimes what is needed is not a new project in prayer, but a fresh look at the way we can pray within our present circumstances or pressures. With two small children to care for, I find that if I sit down, I'm closer to sleep than to prayer. But often I have a sense of God's presence and supportive love.

As a family, towards the end of breakfast (Weetabix scattered, spoons banging), we sing one or two favourite choruses and pray some quick prayers for the day. Emma and Tim enjoy it and it introduces them to a natural way of praying to our heavenly Father.

What matters is to find God's way for us, and to respond to the 'little solitudes' that appear.

For a quiet moment
A 'breathing prayer' for the start of the day:

Breathe in: 'be filled with the Spirit' (Ephesians 5:18).
Breathe out: releasing sin and burdens to God – several times. You may like to thank him as you breathe in, and say: 'Cleanse me, Lord,' as you breathe out.

'Pray as you can, not as you can't.'

John Chapman

GROUP IDEAS

Hands

A leader invites the group to express intercession by using three simple movements.

Hands cupped (as if holding something in them). We give thanks for all God has given us over the past week.
A moment of silence.

Hands reaching out (as if to show God a suffering world). We pray for the world in its suffering and pain.
A moment of silence.

Hands reaching up (as in longing and welcome). We express our hope in God for the world he came to save.
A moment of silence.

GROUP IDEAS

Listening intercessions

Spend the first few minutes in silence. Being still gives God permission to guide our praying. Allow him to give a verse, a picture or a word. Then 'pray it in'. If praying for someone absent from the group, follow through with an encouraging card or letter.

GROUP IDEAS

Prayer walks

In a small group (or as a pair) walk together for half an hour in silence. The idea is to be sensitive to the environment, whether inner-city, suburban or rural. Invariably the silence heightens awareness of the world around. Share impressions. Turn these into prayer together.

With a friend, pray for your street while you walk slowly past each house. Churches are finding that this bears fruit in evangelism as homes are 'soaked' in prayer.

GROUP IDEAS

Letter to God

Although this activity is an obvious choice for an evening group, you can adapt it for other times of meeting.

Each person writes an account of his or her day on paper, with facts, feelings and reflections all thrown in. Allow plenty of time for this activity.

Each person *briefly* shares:
♦ Something to thank God for
♦ A difficult thing (if they want to).

Now pray for one another.

Finally, each person thinks of something learned from the exercise. The leader commits the day into God's hands.

GROUP IDEAS

Pebbles

If possible, place a simple wooden cross in the centre of the group. Put some pebbles in a basket or dish – enough for the group. They can symbolize:
♦ anxiety (1 Peter 5:7)
♦ someone forgiven (Luke 6:14)
♦ a situation to leave behind (Hebrews 12:1-2)

In the context of a talk on any of these areas, invite people to take one of the pebbles. Allow time for them to be able to respond. Perhaps play a tape of quiet music. As part of their prayer, invite them to place their stone at the foot of the cross. This physical gesture is a 'releasing' exercise.

GROUP IDEAS

God in colour

Most people enjoy this exercise. You'll need about ten sheets of coloured writing paper or the sticky-backed coloured paper available from art shops. Choose a mixture of pastels and strong shades. Lay them out on a coffee table.

The leader should stress that there are no right or wrong answers. Pray before you begin.

Invite people to select a colour which 'represents' God. They don't remove the paper – simply name it. So, for example, someone may choose yellow, because God is glorious and powerful.

Give plenty of time. Invite people to share their reasons for their choice of colour. No comments from others in the group!

Allowing slightly more time, invite people to select two or three colours which represent themselves. ('Red because I can be strong and volatile; grey because of my calm, reflective side.') If people are hesitating, the leader should share first. If people don't want to talk, that's fine too.

Ask people to choose a colour which represents a hope connected with something they would like God to do for them – 'Orange, because I know I should be more bold!' The leader should write the responses on a piece of paper.

At the end repeat the list, so that the group can pray for one another. Again, no compulsion to pray aloud.

At the end of this exercise the group may have expressed some very personal reflections; it's helpful if the leader thanks them for being honest and open.

GROUP IDEAS

Journey of life

Give each person a plain A4 (or larger) sheet of paper. Have lots of coloured crayons or felt pens in the middle of the room.

Now invite group members to 'draw their life'. They may want to imagine it as a winding road, sometimes steep, sometimes rocky, sometimes smooth and rolling. Or they may prefer to think of it as a sea voyage; they could chart a course between 'islands' of experience. Select a theme such as special people, major changes, times of growing in faith – all of which can be expressed in visual form. Absolutely no artistic skill is required. This must be stressed! The leader should be sensitive to the fact that many people have areas of pain which still hurt when they look back at them. Be aware – and be available if you see this is too difficult for some. This activity needs prayer beforehand and afterwards.

After twenty minutes or so, people could share their picture (not too lengthily) in twos or threes, followed by praying for one another in the same grouping. The leader can conclude by asking for feedback: 'Did you find it easy to do?'

Allow people to respond briefly, and then commit the group into God's hands, asking for his love to fill memories and lives.

GROUP IDEAS

Pictures

The leader should make a collection of postcard-sized pictures. Some should be specifically 'sacred', but others should be of a more general appeal: country scenes, people, a stately home. You'll need enough for your groups plus a few spare. Spread the pictures on the floor. Give a few minutes for people to choose and then pick up one of the pictures. Ask people to remember (or write down) the reason for their choice. Make sure people realize they can give absolutely *any* reason.

Then allow five minutes for them to ponder on their subject. It may seem a long time, but it allows for reflection. Invite people to say why they chose their picture – encourage them to expand. Often something personal has been triggered and it's good to be able to talk about it. Depending on the size of group, pray for one another in pairs, or in silence.

Symbols and gestures

1. *Symbols and gestures* 'May my prayer be set before you like incense; may the lifting up of my hands be like the evening sacrifice' (Psalm 141:2). See also Revelation 5:8.

In the temple, the psalmist senses help from his prayer of petition. He sees the incense rising to heaven and its aroma reminds him of God's holy presence. He lifts his hands – an outward sign of the inward lifting of his heart to God. This use of body language intensifies his praying.

♦ What symbols or gestures do we use in our Sunday worship?
♦ Have we lost any of them through fear of 'religiosity'?
♦ Share any that help you in your personal prayer.

Mark Stibbe's book, *A Kingdom of Priests*, explains the Old Testament significance of the Temple in the prayer life of God's people. He shows how we can use similar patterns to pray creatively with an understanding of our biblical, Jewish heritage.

2. *Praying the Scriptures* is an ancient and fine tradition. When you read a passage, take one verse and use it as the theme for your praying. What is the benefit of this? It was said of scholar and preacher Dr Martin Lloyd-Jones that people learned as much from his praying as from his preaching.

3. *Play quiet instrumental music* and then read a short passage of Scripture over it. Begin with Matthew 6:25-34. See how the group respond in prayer. Silence may be appropriate. How did music help?

4. *What would Jesus...?* Pray for someone using the question: 'What would Jesus do for her / him?' Allow your imagination to lead you.

Celtic Prayer

The Celtic world is very much in vogue. But beyond its romantic image and New Age popularity lies the reality of the Christian church which was active in these islands in the fourth and fifth centuries. The profound spirituality of those long-ago Christians has a great deal to say to us in the late twentieth century.

Much of what we know about the beginnings of Christianity in the British Isles comes from the pen of St Bede. He completed his *History of the English Church* in 731. He writes of great saints like Aidan and Columba who took the gospel to their people and travelled tirelessly preaching and teaching.

Community matters

The Celtic church was based on monastic communities which fitted well with the rural, tribal nature of society at that time. The monastery would be made up of both men and women, some of whom had taken vows of celibacy, but there were also families attached to the community. From these monasteries, which were natural resource centres, the monks went out to take the gospel to the surrounding areas.

Evangelism was one of the hallmarks of Celtic Christianity. The Celts were less interested in buildings and structures than they were in seeing the transformation of the world for God. A renewed community was at the heart of their vision of a redeemed world. They retained an openness to the world around them and also to God.

One of the marks of this was their willingness to 'wander for the sake of Christ'. The *peregrinati*, as they were known, left their homeland and set out to wander with no thought of where they were going. Their motive was the purification of their souls through discipline and self-denial; this was balanced by their burning desire to preach Christ and to live out the gospel.

They were sometimes given to extremes of self-denial – going without food and praying for long periods in adverse weather – in their desire to know Christ and attain heaven. Another way of understanding this is to recognize their single-mindedness and the practical nature of their discipleship. They were not content with a superficial faith which did not affect their lifestyle.

Christ at the centre

Celtic Christianity was Bible-based. The Celts were not especially interested in theological debate, but they loved the Scriptures, as their beautifully copied manuscripts demonstrate. St Aidan had his monks recite the Psalms as they walked the wilds of Northumbria and later biographers delighted to show how closely the lives of the Celtic saints mirrored those of biblical characters.

The cross, too, was central to the spiritual life of the Celtic church. The great carved high crosses still standing in parts of the British Isles are testimony to this. Often the upper part of the cross is encircled with a ring of stone which may represent in visual form the truth that Christ died for the whole world and that redemption is God's design for all creation. This belief is captured in the title of a book of Celtic prayer by George McCloud, the founder of the modern Iona community: *The Whole Earth Shall Cry Glory* (Wild Goose Publications).

The Celts are often portrayed as being creation-centred in their world view, and indeed they recognized and worshipped

God in and through his creation. But they acknowledged that ours is a fallen world which needs redeeming. They did not worship the elements (such as wind, rain or sea), but the God who created them and who calmed the storm and controlled the wind and the waves.

Rhythm of prayer

One of the most attractive features of Celtic prayer is its rhythmic nature. Many prayers are written in rhyme, sometimes with repeated patterns of three – a reminder of the 'Trinity relationship' at the heart of the Christian faith. Celtic Christianity is firmly based on the Trinity. The Celts spoke of God the Father and creator of the world; of God the Son, the loving friend and risen Lord; and of the Spirit who is at work in the world, pervading all of life with his divine presence and mediating between heaven and earth.

St Patrick wrote:
I bind unto myself today
The strong name of the Trinity
By invocation of the same,
The Three in One, and One in Three.
(Opening lines of the hymn 'St Patrick's Breastplate', Hymns Ancient and Modern Revised.)

All seasons

The Celtic Christians had a deep awareness of the presence of God. They invited him into all their activities and their prayers covered every aspect of life from cradle to grave, from rising and dressing in the morning to lying down at night. They had prayers for lighting the fire, for milking the cow, for working in the fields, for going on a journey. They knew what it meant to 'pray in the Spirit on all occasions with all kinds of prayers and request.' (Ephesians 6:18).

Recognizing God in all things, they could pray:
God shield the house, the fire, the
   kine,
Everyone who dwells here tonight
Shield myself and my beloved group
Preserve us from violence and from
   harm.
(A Carmichael, *New Moon of the Seasons: Prayer from the Highlands and Islands*, Floris Classics)

The Celts' awareness of God had a two-fold aspect. They acknowledged that he is as close to us as the air we breathe, while also recognizing that he is glorious in his majesty, far beyond anything we can imagine. In theological language, they proclaimed both the *immanence* and the *transcendence* of God.

The Celts honoured the incarnation with prayers addressing the tiny helpless baby born to Mary, and they wondered at the Lord of the universe who commanded the wind and waves and set the stars in space.

Praying with variety

Prayers in the Celtic tradition echo today's renewed interest in finding new ways of praying for different people and different situations. Celtic prayer sometimes took the form of silent meditation, perhaps with a visual aid from the natural world. Thus a certain monk could say:

Learned in music sings the lark
I leave my cell to listen;
His open beak spills music, hark!
Where Heaven's bright cloudlets
   glisten.
And so I'll sing my morning psalm
That God bright Heaven may give me
And keep me in eternal calm
And from all sin relieve me.
(R Flower, *The Irish Tradition*)

At other times the Celts appear to 'batter the gates of heaven' with fervent prayers against the power of evil at work in the world. Their love of solitude and silence

In the circle of his love

stemmed from a desire to turn aside in order to communicate with God more fully. St Cuthbert spent ten years in solitude on the Farne Islands before reluctantly returning to the mainland to become a bishop.

Into battle

The Celts were acutely aware of the supernatural and of the power of evil. They were familiar with what we sometimes call spiritual warfare. Physical combat was something which was a regular part of warring tribal society, and the Celts realized that there were battles to be fought in the spiritual realm also.

They transferred the language of battle into their prayers. On one occasion St Patrick, who was so influential in the conversion of Ireland, was engaged in a spiritual battle with the druid advisors of the High King of Tara. He and his companions lit the paschal fire on their return to Ireland on the night of the druidical feast of Tara. As a druid approached Patrick reviling the Trinity and the Christian faith, Patrick prayed in a loud voice that God would destroy him. As he called out verses of Scripture, there was upheaval in the

natural world – an earthquake. The story illustrates the need to be confident in God and to find strength in the risen Christ:

At Tara today in this fateful hour
I place all Heaven with its power,
And the sun with its brightness
And the snow with its whiteness
And fire with all the strength it hath
And lightning with its rapid wrath...
All these I place
By God's almighty help and grace,
Between myself and the powers of
*   darkness.*
(W P Marsh and C Bamford,
Celtic Christianity, Ecology and
Holiness, Floris Classics)

Encircled by God

The Celts had special prayers of protection called *caims*, or encircling prayers. They would draw a circle around themselves as they prayed, to illustrate the protecting power of God surrounding them. These are among the most popular type of Celtic prayers used by Christians today:

Circle me Lord
Keep protection near
And danger afar

Circle me Lord
Keep hope within
Keep doubt without

Circle me Lord

Keep light near
And darkness afar

Circle me Lord
Keep peace within
Keep evil out.
(David Adam, *The Edge of Glory,*
Triangle)

Similarly loricae (breastplate prayers) expressed the conviction that God is both mighty and near at hand to protect his people. The most famous of this kind of prayer is 'St Patrick's Breastplate', already quoted and still sung in churches today.

GROUP IDEAS

Doing the dishes

The Celts prayed about everything. They made God welcome in every aspect of their lives, however mundane. A Celt might pray while milking the cow – would today's equivalent task be a trip to the supermarket? What ordinary tasks in your daily life could be transformed by asking God to be present as you do them? Here are a few suggestions:

♦ waiting for the bus
♦ preparing a meal
♦ doing housework
♦ weeding the garden

In pairs write a simple prayer asking for God's presence in your chosen task.

GROUP IDEAS

Bible echoes

When later Christians remembered the Celtic saints they looked for aspects of their lives which echoed stories from the Bible. So for example, St Cuthbert was called from tending sheep in the same way that David was called as a shepherd boy in the Bible.

♦ Think together in your group of ways in which your own lives and the life of your church or fellowship group echo passages from the Bible. What lessons can you learn?

GROUP IDEAS

Prayerscapes

If you live in or near a city or town, compose a prayer in the Celtic style about an aspect of its life. If you live in the countryside, compose a prayer about a feature of the landscape which moves you to think of God. Do this in twos or threes.

GROUP IDEAS

One of the prayers in David Adam's book *The Edge of Glory* is called 'Affirmations' and is designed for communal use.

A leader says: 'I believe O God of all gods that you are...', thus affirming God's eternal presence among us. Then after a pause (or the beat of a drum or tambourine), someone else from the group responds: 'The eternal Father of...', inserting a word expressing one of God's attributes such as love, peace, mercy and so on. After another pause, the leader starts again and a different member of the group contributes the response.

After the time of prayer you might like to share in the group why you chose your particular description of God and say what it means to you.

GROUP FOCUS

GROUP IDEAS

Three lines

♦ Compose a simple three-line prayer with the following framework, adding your own ending to each line:

    Creator ...
    Saviour ...
    Sanctifier ...

♦ This prayer can be spoken by three people or by three groups.

♦ What other names would you choose to compose a threefold prayer to the Trinity?

GROUP IDEAS

Write a prayer

David Adam's *Power Lines* (Triangle) contains modem prayers in the Celtic style about work. One of them begins:

Lord I have seen a crane lift a heavy load.
Lift me, Lord,
Out of darkness into light
Out of despair into joy
Out of doubt into hope.

In pairs, follow this pattern to make up your own rhythmic prayers based on the world around you:

Lord I have seen...
Lift me, Lord,
Out of....

GROUP IDEAS

A prayer to close:

The Trinity
Protecting me
The Father be
Over me
The Saviour be
Under me
The Spirit be
About Me
The Holy Three
Defending me
As evening comes
Bless my home
Holy Three
Watching me
As shadows fall
Hear my call
Sacred Three
Encircle me
So it may be
Amen to Thee
Holy Three
About me

(David Adam, *The Edge of Glory*, Triangle)

GROUP IDEAS

Encircling prayer

Try saying the encircling prayer quoted above with the encircling action. One way to do this is to stretch out one arm in front of you and draw a circle around your head, symbolizing the enfolding of God.

Journeying on

1. The Celts encouraged each other on their spiritual journeys by forming one-to-one relationships for that purpose. It was a common practice to have an *anamchara*, or 'soul friend'. Is there someone whom you would consider already to be your soul friend? If not, is there someone who could fulfil this role? It is a relationship of equals, two people walking side by side for prayer and encouragement. Ask God to give you a soul friend and to enable you to be a soul friend to someone.

2. Many Celtic prayers were addressed to the Trinity and composed in lines of three. Think about how you normally address your prayers. Is it to the Father, the Son or the Spirit? What does this say about your image of God? Try spending a week addressing a different member of the Trinity in your times of prayer.

3. Are there ways in which you can be like the *peregrinati* when you go out into the community? Next time you visit the shops or walk down your street ask God to make you aware of him in each encounter and see who he brings across your path.

4. The Celtic Christians were responsible for preserving art and culture as well as the faith in the troubled times of invasions during the eighth and ninth centuries. Poetry and the visual arts were important parts of their daily lives and of their worship. How could poetry and the visual arts enrich the prayer and worship of your own life and that of your church?

5. Find time to go out into the open air to pray and allow the elements to speak to you of God and of your relationship with him.

YOUR COMMENTS

Ignatian Prayer

Ignatius Loyola was born into the Spanish nobility at the end of the fourteenth century. As a young man he was a soldier. He was wounded in 1521 and abandoned his military career, determining to become a soldier of Christ. He is best remembered as the founder of the Society of Jesus (the Jesuits) and as the author of the *Spiritual Exercises*, his in-depth guidebook to the spiritual life: it remains immensely influential four hundred years after his death.

At the heart of Ignatian prayer (prayer in the style of Ignatius) is the contemplation of the life of Jesus in Scripture in order to receive his grace and follow him. It involves using our senses and imagination to enter more fully into God's presence. We tend to restrict prayer to words – the Ignatian approach encourages us to take a much wider view.

Head and heart gap

Often there is a gap between our head and our heart. We know what we should think and believe, but our heart says differently. We know in our head that God loves us unconditionally, but our heart is often full of other messages: 'Would God love me if he really knew what I'm like?' But it is in that deep, inner experience of our hearts that God wants to meet us.

Senses and imagination

Most often we approach God through words. But we have also been given our senses and our imagination. The psalmist says: '*Taste* and see that the Lord is good' (Psalm 34:8).

So we might, for example, imagine putting ourselves in the place of the different people who came to Jesus to be healed. Instead of thinking of physical ailments, we might think of ourselves as being spiritually blind, deaf, paralyzed or covered with the leprosy of sin. We can imagine ourselves coming to Jesus and having him reach out and touch us and heal us. Imagination can make this very vivid. We can experience a true encounter with Jesus as a result of this prayer.

The events in the life of Jesus can become so alive that we experience the presence of Jesus here and now in our midst. Such an encounter with God is the purpose of Ingatian prayer.

'Perhaps some rare individuals experience God through abstract contemplation alone, most of us need to be more deeply rooted in the senses. We must not despise this simpler, more humble route into God's presence.' (Richard Foster, *Celebration of Discipline*, Hodder and Stoughton)

How do we pray?

I believe that it is important to remember that the initiative in prayer is always God's and never our own. Christian prayer is a response, not a pursuit.

The prophet Hosea pictures God as a lover yearning for relationship with his people: 'Therefore I am now going to allure her; I will lead her into the desert and speak tenderly to her' (Hosea 2:14). Similarly God wants to take us into the desert place, the dry and barren places within us, perhaps an area of loneliness, fear, discouragement or shame. It is in such a place that he longs to 'speak tenderly' to us.

Becoming still

The psalmist says, 'Be still and know that I am God' (Psalm 46:10). If I am to recognize God in my life, I must learn to be still. This is extremely difficult! It is important to remember that God's thoughts

are not our thoughts (Isaiah 55:8). I need to let go of my inner clamour and clutter, and of my confined way of seeing, in order to see things from God's perspective.

Here are four simple aids to stillness:

1. *'Familiar chair'* In his book *Hidden Fire* Brother Ramon observes that just as people in love 'always manage to find a place to be alone together, to be lost in each other's presence and to enter into loving, intimate communion', so we can find such a place in our relationship with God. This 'familiar chair' is the place where our relationship with God can deepen. It becomes a prayer-saturated sanctuary.

2. *Visual aid* Use a candle, flowers or a cross as a focus for your thoughts.

3. *Music*

4. *Comfortable position* Start off by breathing deeply and relaxing, stilling our restless bodies. This is not like Yoga which involves emptying the mind. Here it is about being filled as I realize God is here with me. I might echo Acts 17:28 by repeating, 'In God I live and move and have my being' as I become aware of the life of God within me.

Use of repetition

Many traditional forms of prayer are very repetitive – for example, the Jesus prayer ('Jesus, Son of God, have mercy on me, a sinner.'). Many of these prayers began as pilgrim prayers. When walking it is more difficult to concentrate the mind than when still, but the constant repetition in time with our step or breathing can induce an inner stillness in which we become aware of God's presence.

The important thing is that I focus my attention upon God's presence with me now. God is where I am. That is so obvious, but often we think of God as being 'out there' instead of 'right here'!

Reading Scripture

Before the monks had their own individual Bibles, the abbot would gather the brothers together to read Scripture to them. When a verse or phrase stood out to a particular monk, he would slip away to his room to meditate on it.

We too can read a passage of Scripture several times, letting it wash over us, and see if any word or phrase stands out. Gerard Hughes describes the process of musing on Scripture as being like 'sucking a boiled sweet'! We don't analyze what the sweet is made up of – we simply enjoy it.

Personalizing Scripture

We might read Isaiah 43:1-4 and find that the phrase 'You are precious and honoured in my sight' stands out. We might ask, what does it mean to be honoured by God?

I remember a mum telling me that when she asked that question she remembered her own father who, when seeing her off on the train, would always doff his hat. This conjured up for her a sense of being honoured, a deep display of courtesy. It gave her an insight of God's attitude to her: 'You are honoured.' It is possible to personalize many verses of Scripture and to receive them as though 'written for me'.

Distractions

Sooner or later, and probably sooner, our minds will become distracted. 'I wonder what's for dinner?' will mingle with the word or phrase of Scripture which attracts you.

Instead of seeing these distractions as intrusions, let them become part of our prayer. A phrase or verse from the Bible can be like a searchlight which highlights my thoughts, memories, fears and ambitions.

The author of Genesis wrote: 'Now the earth was formless and empty, darkness was over the surface of the deep, and the Spirit of God was hovering over the waters' (Genesis 1:2). When I pray from Scripture I am letting the Spirit of God hover over the darkness and chaos of my being. Distractions do not refer so much to our thoughts, but to the direction of our thinking. If your thoughts are turned to worries, hopes, longings, temptations and guilt, then let the Word of God speak into your everyday preoccupations.

On one occasion I was trying to meditate on the passage which relates Jesus appearing to the disciples and Thomas in the upper room after his resurrection (John 20:24-20). I was unable to concentrate because my mind was buzzing with all the things I had to do – and

in particular with thoughts of a friend who had attempted suicide. As I brought these preoccupations to Jesus I saw, more vividly than ever before, his disfigured hands. Not neat, nail-shaped holes, but wounds gashed and scarred, and in his side an unsightly scar. I saw that Jesus stood with me, to bring peace in the midst of deformity, ugliness and pain.

Imaginative contemplation

The Ignatian form of prayer and meditation encourages the use of imagination with Scripture. Gerard Hughes writes: 'It is the imagination that projects into our conscious minds, thoughts, memories and feelings which although hidden from us in our subconscious, are in fact influencing our perception, thinking and acting – including our perception of God.' (*Oh God, Why?* Bible Reading Fellowship)

We may, for example, think of Jesus with his disciples in the boat when the storm blew up. We may imagine ourselves in the boat as the waves beat against the sides threatening to overturn it. 'Where is Jesus? Why isn't

he there when I need him?' – such thoughts may surface, reflecting a subconscious fear that God won't be there when we need him. Such fears can then be met with God's truth: he promises his people that he will not 'fail you or forsake you' (1 Chronicles 28:20).

Imaginative prayer is especially suited to gospel passages.

1. Read the passage several times until it is familiar to you.

2. Imagine the event is happening now and that you are a participant, active in the scene. Do not worry if your imagination does not present the scene vividly. If you find it difficult to enter the scene, imagine you are trying to describe it to a child, making it as vivid as possible.

3. It can help attentiveness to ask yourself of any scene: who is present; what are they doing; what are they saying; am I an onlooker; do I identify with one particular character?

4. If distractions come let them enter the gospel scene.

They may draw you deeper into it.

5. Talk with the character in the scene. Talk to Christ or to the Father. Always speak from the heart, simply and honestly.

6. Ask for what you desire.

7. Do not worry if your mind keeps straying from the scene. When you become conscious of inattention, gently bring yourself back to the scene.

Review of prayer

At the end of the exercise, it is helpful to review what happened during that time. Not so much 'What ideas did I have?', but 'What did the Lord show me? What did I feel about what went on?'

It may be the Lord is inviting you to go back to a point when you were either moved or stuck. Ignatius says: 'I should remain quietly meditating upon a point until I have been satisfied, that is until the insight has been completed, the struggle resolved – for now.'

What if I have no imagination?

Some people think they have no imagination. Try visualizing the place where you ordinarily go to look for your post in the morning. Have a good look at it, and then pick up the mail and check it for bills or personal letters.... In doing so, your imagination has been released. Ignatius is asking no more than that.

Should we trust our imagination?

Some have objected to using the imagination out of a concern that it is untrustworthy and could be used by the devil. Such concern is justifiable. Like all our faculties, the imagination is part of our sinful nature. But just as God can redeem our reason (fallen as it is) and use it for good, so God can redeem our imagination, which he has created and allows to speak to us.

Another understandable worry is that an over-active imagination may lead to self-deception. For this reason it is vitally important at the outset to invite God to fill us with his presence and to ask him that we may desire his truth and his ways.

We must test everything against Scripture. If imagination contradicts Scripture we bring our imagination into line with God's truth. After all, Scripture is the prime reason for imaginative prayer.

Jesus taught by making constant appeal to the imagination in his parables. The imagination enables us to come to God with mind and heart.

GROUP IDEAS

Be still

- ◆ Practise becoming still.
- ◆ Breathe in and out slowly – breathing in the name of Jesus and breathing out the cares and business of the day.
- ◆ Repeat the Jesus Prayer or a Scripture-based statement such as 'In Him I live and move and have my being' (Acts 17:28) – so that you become increasingly aware of God's presence.
- ◆ Allow God to show you his love – perhaps by an impression or picture, or simply through awareness. Don't worry if you feel nothing. Believe facts, not feelings: 'Come near to God and he will come near to you' (James 4:8).

GROUP IDEAS

In the picture

Read the story of the Good Samaritan (Luke 10:25-37).

- ◆ First try to imagine yourself as the priest who passes by on the other side of the road. What reason could you give for not getting involved?
- ◆ Next try to imagine yourself as the person who fell among the robbers and who was left half-dead on the roadside. What might you think as you see people pass by, ignoring your cries for help?
- ◆ Thirdly, imagine yourself as the Samaritan. Try to envisage some situation today where you could act as a Good Samaritan to others in trouble.

GROUP IDEAS

What may I do for you?

- ◆ Become still, welcoming God's presence.
- ◆ Pray, asking God to direct your heart and thoughts towards him.
- ◆ Ask a group member to read Mark 10:46-52 aloud. Ask him or her to repeat the reading.
- ◆ Spend some time in quiet, imagining the scene.
- ◆ Try to imagine the excitement of the crowd: Jesus is coming!
- ◆ Think of the heat, the dust, the noise. See blind Bartimaeus who hears that Jesus of Nazareth is passing: 'Jesus, Son of David, have pity on me!'
- ◆ Imagine yourself as the blind man – how do you feel?
- ◆ Then Jesus asks: 'What do you want me to do for you?' What is your response to that question?

GROUP IDEAS

Called by name

Open your Bible at Isaiah 43:1-7.

- ◆ Spend a few moments becoming still, welcoming God's presence.
- ◆ Invite one member of the group to read the passage aloud. Pause and read it again silently.
- ◆ Re-read until a verse or phrase stands out. You may like to reflect on the statement 'I have called you by name'. What name does God give you? How do you feel about God calling you by name?
- ◆ What are the waters you fear may sweep over you? Can you receive God's word, 'I will be with you'?
- ◆ Speak to God about what he has shown you. You may wish to share your reflections with others in the group.

Going further

1. Take a few moments to think about some of your favourite places – a beautiful garden, a special seaside place, outside your local bakery with the wonderful aroma of newly baked bread wafting out. What makes them special?

Do you take time each day to enjoy the colours, sounds, textures and smells of things around you? Or do you rush past them and miss the wonderful ways they speak of God the Creator. Why do you rush so much?

*To see a World in a Grain of Sand
And a Heaven in a Wild Flower,
Hold Infinity in the palm of your hand,
And Eternity in an hour.*
William Blake, *Auguries of Innocence*

Take a few minutes of quiet to notice the people and things around you – the feel of a chair, the colour of people's clothes, the sounds of their voices. How does it feel to stop, look, listen, touch and smell?

2. Ignatius valued silence. He knew the importance of simply being still and acknowledging the presence of our loving God.

♦ Take a few moments now to be still....
♦ How did that feel?
♦ What things stop you from taking time to be still?
♦ Are you afraid of silence?

3. Ignatius believed that 'all things in this world are gifts of God, created for us, to be the means by which we can come to know him better, love him more surely, and serve him more faithfully.' (David Fleming SJ, *The Spiritual Exercises of St Ignatius – a Contemporary Reading*)

So nothing we encounter is wasted. It is easy to see how this can apply to the good things we encounter. What about the difficult things? What about illness, redundancy, exam failure, being burgled? How can these provide an opportunity to know and love God better?

4. Take a few moments to be quiet and think over the last twenty-four hours. What did you enjoy? Re-live those enjoyable aspects in your imagination. They are God's gifts to you, signs of his love.

Nothing is too mundane to thank God for: think of the running water you use each day, think of the sun shining, think of letters or a phone call. These things draw you to God.

You may also remember things about which you feel uncomfortable, moments which turned you away from God. Allow them to serve as opportunities to turn afresh to God as you ask for, and receive, forgiveness.

Do you think that a regular review of the day like this could help you?

Ideas from Taizé

Do you recognize this? This distinctive cross comes from the ecumenical community of Taizé in the Burgundy region of France. Its shape, suggesting a dove in flight as well as a cross, tells in a graphic way that reconciliation and peace are God's gifts to his people, gifts which must be accepted and lived out day to day.

Since its foundation, the community of Taizé has sought to be a place of pilgrimage, reconciliation and peace. It is a place to search for God and to find in Christ the meaning to life. The community's founder, Brother Roger, says that Taizé 'aims at being both in the world and in the heart of the church, fully awake to the tragedy of Christian disunity.' The brothers aim to live out the beatitudes in their daily lives.

Worship is the heartbeat of the community. Three times a day in the Church of Reconciliation the brothers and pilgrims join together in prayer. This is fundamental to Taizé's commitment to 'common faith and the power of Christ to bring together and unite'.

What is Taizé?
Roger Schutz founded the ecumenical community in Taizé in 1940. Today there are more than ninety brothers, both Protestant and Catholic, from over twenty different countries. Not all of them live in Taizé. Small fraternities are to be found amongst the poor all over the world. By living among them the brothers seek to identify with them and to be signs of reconciliation.

From small beginnings Taizé has grown to be a meeting place for pilgrims from around the world. Young people, and the not-so-young, have been flocking there since the end of the 1950s. Today during the summer months there are often 6000 or more visitors each week.

What happens at Taizé?
Pilgrims usually come to Taizé for a week at a time. They come seeking peace and simplicity in their search for God, and for direction and meaning in their lives. These week-long meetings 'aim to explore all that nourishes our faith and leads to reflection on how to unite prayer and daily life'. The community's daily pattern provides opportunities for listening, discussion, prayer and reflection in large meetings, small groups and alone. On Friday evenings there is prayer around the cross. Evening prayer on Saturday is a candlelit Paschal vigil which is followed by Sunday morning Eucharist. Worship at Taizé interweaves many strands: music and chants, silences, spoken prayer, readings, candles and icons are all part of the pattern.

Taizé worship
Prayer The community recognizes that prayer is a vitally important part of our Christian growth. Taizé encourages people to experiment with different forms of prayer. In being exposed to new ways of praying we can surprise ourselves with our own responses. It may help us out of a rut. It may help us to be in touch with God in a new way. Perhaps it may help us to express our deep feelings for God and about God.

Music Taizé's distinctive style of chanting has become world-famous. Singing is a way of praying and a few words or phrases repeated again and again reinforce the quality of that prayer. The Taizé chants are written with great simplicity of words and music to enable all to join in, regardless of language. I find their repetitiveness helpful, although I know not everybody does. One young adult put it this way: 'the chants are sung over and over again until eventually you find yourself no longer concentrating on singing the music, but on talking to God through the music.'

After my husband died I found myself playing Taizé tapes a great deal. They made possible a way of communicating with God when I felt completely empty of prayer. Now when I'm feeling down or harassed, or when things seem to be getting too much, I find that playing Taizé music has a calming effect. It enables me to pause, to turn away from myself, to meet God and let him touch my innermost being.

Silence On of the things I find appealing about Taizé prayer is the lengthy silences. Long periods of quiet in the company of others can be a most enriching experience. We are so unaccustomed to it that many may find keeping silence difficult and uncomfortable. Being silent is not about emptying our minds of all thoughts. It is a much more active and creative process, in which we open ourselves with childlike trust to allow God to enter our deepest being. When we first met to worship in this way we kept quite a short time of silence. In subsequent meetings we were able to lengthen it gradually until it lasted about ten minutes.

Candles Many people find it a great help to have a 'visual aid' when praying. I find my prayer enhanced by using a lighted candle to help focus my concentration. A candle reminds us that Christ is the light of the world and in him there is no darkness at all. Christ's love is a fire that never dies. In experimenting with Taizé worship in the parish we used candles – lots of them placed in the shape of a cross. But a word of warning: candles (or, alternatively, night-lights) have a way of leaking their wax and it's no fun trying to get it off the church carpet! Stand them in deep saucers or dishes.

Icons are visual images which help us to focus our attention on God the Father, on Christ and on the Holy Spirit. Some banners could be considered a modern form of icon. Images can speak powerfully and be instrumental in developing a deeper understanding of God. Icons can be particularly helpful in times of meditation and silence. Most Christian bookshops have a selection of icons and other pictures.

Readings A 'Letter from Taizé' is published six times a year. It includes writings from one of the Brothers, and Bible passages for daily reading and meditation. These 'Johannine Hours', as they are called, developed as times of silence and sharing around the Word of God. They grew out of a need for spiritual nourishment in the midst of daily life. The letter is available by subscription from the Taizé Community, 71250 Cluny, France.

The readings are suitable for both individual and group use. After the silence and the meditation, the group comes together for discussion and prayer. Communicate to others what has brought you joy from the meditation. The aim is that

Paths of reconciliation

'the Johannine Hours allow us to hear the harmonious melody, which is none other than the voice of Christ who loves us. If we listen in our hearts to the Word of God, and assimilate it in our life so as to put in into practice, then we will truly be blessed.'

Colour and depth have been added to the experience when this sharing has been in an ecumenical context. It has been a means of increasing my knowledge and understanding of other Christian traditions. Ignorance is often the cause of disunity. We need to use all possible means to open the channels of reconciliation.

Listening with the Heart (Cassell) provides useful resources for sessions of contemplation and sharing around the Word of God.

Making adaptations

If you are going to use Taizé-style worship in private devotions, in groups or larger gatherings, you need to be sensitive in adapting it to the time and place of use. The community is very concerned that pilgrims should not try to set up replicas of Taizé worship when they return home.

Reconciliation

Returning pilgrims are encouraged to live as signs of reconciliation, as salt and light, in their own communities. Right from its inception Taizé has worked to open paths of reconciliation between Christians. As we use forms of Taizé prayer and worship so we too need to concentrate on finding ways to be signs of reconciliation in the places where we live and work. Reconciliation is not an aim in itself. Once reconciled, Christians are to become a haven of peace and trust for all. If we remain unreconciled, how can we be a reflection of the God of love? Each of us is called to become involved where we live and to be a person of reconciliation there, to build trust across the chasms between peoples of different cultures and traditions.

Reconciliation isn't only about trying to bring together the different Christian denominations, or of bringing about peace in Bosnia, the Middle East or Northern Ireland. It is also about bringing together and finding peace in families and between friends, neighbours and communities.

On a personal level, using Taizé

prayer for reconciliation has encouraged me to see that individuals and small groups can make a difference. Corporate prayer helps me to pray for the large scale needs, but it also helps me focus on the need for reconciliation on a smaller more local level.

Even at times when humanity seems to be heading for disaster, individuals have found a way to see beyond personal conflicts and to cross barriers of denomination, race and nationality. Each one of us has the capacity to be that individual who makes a difference. Forgiveness is a very personal step. It involves showing kindness, risking being misunderstood and expecting nothing in return. Reconciliation is something we have to work at. In the words of Brother Roger: 'The call to reconciliation leaves us exposed. Loving, forgiving those who are opposed to us is a miracle in our lives.'

God forgives us and loves us unconditionally. Do we have the courage to love enough to forgive others? Can we afford not to?

GROUP IDEAS

Making a difference

As a group try working through the following check list as a way of focusing on the practical issues of reconciliation:

♦ When making important decisions about my way of life have I put God first?
♦ Have I prayed regularly?
♦ Do I really love God's name? Have I been guilty of foul language or of contempt for God's name?
♦ Whom have I upset today, this week?
♦ Did I shout at my children, my family, my co-workers for no good reason?
♦ Have I been truthful and fair? Have I deliberately deceived others? Judged them rashly? Injured their reputations?

GROUP IDEAS

Open invitation

As a group discuss how you could move on in commitment to reconciliation.

♦ Have we ever attended a service of another denomination?
♦ Have we taken steps to learn about and understand someone else's spiritual viewpoint?
♦ Are all the members of our group from the same church or denomination?
♦ Have we thought of inviting people from another Christian tradition to take part in our activities?

GROUP IDEAS

Getting started

A basic resource One of the most popular resources for groups is *Songs and Prayers from* Taizé (Cassell); a cassette of twenty of the songs featured in it is also available. Depending on the time available the worship can be adapted – using chants or not; allowing short or long silences; making use of candles and icons. The intercessions can be meaningful and helpful when incorporated into worship services.

Essential equipment A few people in our church wanted to experience more of Taizé worship. Most people knew one or two chants. None of us played an instrument. So I made use of a tape recorder and made a collection of a few well-known chants. I chose chants in English because our folk said they couldn't understand foreign languages. As the group became more familiar with the chants, we used the tape recorder less.

Larger gatherings In most places there are now regular gatherings for Taizé-style worship. Some are based on local churches, while others are planned as special events which seek to attract people from a wide area. It is well worth seeking out such gatherings and joining in. The feel and atmosphere of a larger gathering can be very different from a smaller more intimate group.

Taking it further

YOUR COMMENTS

The following are ways in which some individuals and groups have used Taizé prayer.

Prayer of reconciliation has been offered in Sheffield on a monthly basis for about fifteen years. This gathering was started by students following a visit to Taizé. They wanted to continue sharing prayer together. Sometimes as many as fifty people attend. Before starting the prayer, which progresses without announcements, they sing through the chants so everyone has a chance to learn them.

These meetings have given birth to informal gatherings for singing practice and learning new chants.

For a period of time there was a mid-month gathering as well as the established end-of-month meetings mentioned above. These were times of pilgrimage when the group went out to different places in the diocese. Meeting away from the city centre gave more people in the local area an opportunity to be involved in Taizé prayer.

One city parish sets aside time in Advent and in Lent to have a mid-week gathering for Taizé prayer. These meetings are open to all – to people from the parish and from beyond.

One group of busy housewives found that they could only manage to meet once a month, but each person set aside a weekly time to read and meditate alone on the agreed readings. They met monthly to share what God had been saying to them through his Word.

The sayings of Brother Roger

God could do without our prayer. It is a mystery that he sets such store by it.

A fire burning in the human heart, a light in the darkness, Christ loves you as if you were his sole concern. He has given his life for you. That is his secret.

The joy of Easter brings healing to the secret wounds of the soul. It does not make the heart proud. It goes straight to the gateways of light.

God, too dazzling to be seen, becomes visible, yes visible, through the communion in the Body of Christ, his Church.

Do not be dismayed when the essential seems to remain hidden from your eyes. That only makes you more eager than ever to go on towards the One who is risen.

If you pray, it is because of love; if you struggle to restore humanity to those mistreated, that too is because of love.

God never places us in the time of fear, but in the time of trust. The gospel does not regard human beings with pessimism.

Peace of heart is a mainstay of the inner life; it sustains us as we make our way upward towards joy.

Will you let an inner life that has neither beginning nor end, grow within you? There, you stand at the threshold of the gospel's joy, where human solidarities plunge their roots.

Consider you neighbours not just at particular phases of their existence but through all the stages of their life.

God is never an indifferent witness to human affliction; God suffers with each person. There is a pain that God experiences, a suffering felt by Christ.

Being racked with worry has never been a way of living the gospel. Founding our faith on torment would mean building our house on sand.

Intercessory Prayer

The word intercession derives from two Latin words: *inter* (between) and *cedo* (I go). An intercessor, therefore, is a go-between. When we intercede, we stand between two realities: on the one hand the reality of sin, the world and the devil, and, on the other, the reality of God and his rule of love and righteousness. That's the 'collision' we're involved in every time we say the Lord's Prayer.

Relationship and response

Intercession belongs firmly in the Jewish / Christian tradition. It is not about the magical manipulation of divine powers. It's not about placating God to keep him quiet, or about submitting to a fixed and unbending will.

Rather, its purpose is to bring us close enough to God for there to be dialogue between us, a dialogue in which we may 'interfere' in his right to judge us as we immerse those for whom we pray in his tender love and mercy.

In the Old Testament

The Old Testament shows that God's will is not set in solid concrete. He is responsive, generous and willing to 'change his mind'.

Hear the words of Jeremiah: 'If at any time I announce that a nation or kingdom is to be uprooted..., and if that nation I warned repents of its evil, then I will relent and not inflict on it the disaster I had planned' (Jeremiah 18:7,8).

See God's reluctance to judge the people of Sodom and Gomorrah (Genesis 18:20-21) and then his willingness to engage with Abraham's audacious bartering for their salvation. See how he relents from destroying Nineveh when the people turned from their evil ways because of Jonah's – albeit reluctant – intervention (Jonah 3).

But what about Samuel's words: 'He who is the glory of Israel does not lie or change his mind; for he is not a man that he should change his mind' (1 Samuel 15:29)? This might seem to contradict the verses above. On the contrary, it suggests that God is not fickle but faithful, *as well as* being supple and sensitive.

Intercession belongs in the context of a covenant relationship bearing God's seal of promise: 'I will take you as my own people, and I will be your God' (Exodus 6:7). Although obedience is part of the commitment and rebellion is punished, God delights in mercy. He has decided to love because he is love. In his character 'love and faithfulness meet together, righteousness and peace kiss each other' (Psalm 85:10).

Open to debate

This leads to clear convictions that God is open to debate and willing to be 'reminded' of his promise, his character and commitment. Although the people of God were always flagrantly disobeying, as we do now, yet it was God's intention from the outset that there should always be a forgiven and restored community. In Old Testament times this was achieved in two ways:

1. Sacrifice: '...without the shedding of blood there is no forgiveness' (Hebrews 9:22).

2. Mediation: Without a mediator there was no one to represent the people to God and God to the people.

God's people followed careful laws regarding the practice of sacrifice, and God would search

34

for an intercessor with and through whom he could communicate. This was the go-between – the person who stood in the gap, arguing Israel's case to God and being his mouthpiece to them. It is very moving to look at how such men as Abraham, Moses, Solomon, Daniel, Ezra and Nehemiah worshipped God and conversed with him. They repented for the sins of the people, even offering their own lives as a sacrifice if that would shield the people from judgement and restore them to prosperity and peace. They were the friends of God (Exodus 32, 1 Kings 8, Daniel 9, Ezra 9, Nehemiah 1).

The go-between God

Eventually, God gave his only Son to be both the sacrifice and the mediator. Jesus, the 'go-between God', inaugurated a new covenant. He is the new and living way by which all are saved who come to God by him. No further sacrifice for sin is required. Furthermore, Jesus is now raised to a position of authority before the Father where he is continually making intercession for us.

So what part do we play now? Romans 8 presents us with the present picture.

Christ Jesus, who died – more than that, who was raised to life – is at the right hand of God and is also interceding for us. (Romans 8:34) Jesus continues the work of intercession in his position of authority.

You, however, are controlled not by the sinful nature but by the Spirit, if the Spirit of God lives in you. And if anyone does not have the Spirit of Christ, he does not belong to Christ. (Romans 8:9) If the Spirit of God lives in us we belong to Christ.

… the creation itself will be liberated from its bondage to decay and brought into the glorious freedom of the children of God. (Romans 8:21) We know the glorious freedom of the children of God.

Not only so, but we ourselves, who have the firstfruits of the Spirit, groan inwardly as we wait eagerly for our adoption as sons, the redemption of our bodies.' (Romans 8:23) This work is no longer for an elite few; it is the privilege of all Christians to pray and eagerly await God's redemption.

In the same way, the Spirit helps us in our weakness. We do not know what we ought to pray for, but the

Spirit himself intercedes for us with groans that words cannot express. And he who searches our hearts knows the mind of the Spirit, because the Spirit intercedes for the saints in accordance with God's will. (Romans 8:26-27) We are called to participate with Jesus in his intercession for the restoration of all creation. If we don't know how or what to pray it doesn't matter. The Spirit makes prayer out of our wordless sighs and aching groans and these are gathered into the intercession of Jesus himself.

'He who prays stands at that point of intersection where the love of God and the tensions and sufferings we inflict on each other meet and are held to the healing power of God.'

Mother Mary Clare SLG.

The place of intercession

Standing at the intersection

Metropolitan Anthony is the leader of Britain's Russian Orthodox Christians. He likens intercession to standing in 'the eye of the hurricane'. It's the point where all the conflicting forces of tension and violence, meet and with such a force that they hold one another in balance. It is in that breaking point that the crucified and risen Jesus stands beckoning us to join him in his intercession.

As you are drawn to pray from love and compassion instead of self interest, a number of things may happen.

1. You may want to tell God everything in a torrent of words, cries and questions. If you are on your own or in a trusted prayer cell you can let it all out.

2. You may want to repent on behalf of others, owning the sin and showing deep sorrow for it.

3. Words may run out. Simply be silent. Hold up the ones you are praying for to the love of God and soak them in that love until you feel released from doing so.

4. Tears may well up or burst upon you, unbidden. You can be sure that tears spring from the heart of God who is acquainted with grief and pained by the suffering, injustice and perversion he sees. If you cannot cry outwardly, Richard Foster recommends that you have 'a weeping heart' and 'keep your soul in tears'.

5. A willingness to listen may also enable God to give a prophetic word from Scripture, a picture or an idea. If this is the case, don't rush on as if you hadn't heard, but think about it and let it guide you. In all of this we want love's best. It may be appropriate to offer a readiness to work for what we are praying – to give a little, to risk a little, to bring the answers about. For example, in praying for someone's healing I may be asked to go and pray with that person – or to offer to hold his or her hand through long hours of pain.

George Muller spoke of 'gaining a place of intercession' for the orphans in his care through being the one to forego food if there was not enough to go round.

GROUP IDEAS

Hiddenness

Intercession is a largely hidden activity. Jesus hid himself away to pray. Explore the hidden moments of Jesus' life: Matthew 4:1-11; Mark 1:35; 6:46; 14:32; Luke 6:12; 9:28.

1. How do these times compare with the public man in daily ministry?

2. What was happening before and after some of those interludes?

3. How does 'hiddenness' contrast with the qualities our society holds dear?

4. Are you happy with the extent to which you, your group, your church draws aside to pray?

5. Consider the possibility of a half-day or day of prayer in somebody's home at regular intervals – weekly, monthly, termly. People can come and go according to the time they can give.

GROUP IDEAS

Our present sufferings

Calling to mind 'our present sufferings', let your thoughts range over situations in the news, and people or faces known to you who are groaning in pain, decay or bondage.

Hold them before God believing that the Spirit is praying within you desiring God to heal, free and transform.

GROUP IDEAS

Praying generously

Paul's prayers for the churches are an inspiration. They are not limited by his personality or by his frailty. They are fired by and rooted in that extraordinary love of God which bears all things, believes all things, hopes all things and never gives up.

Look at Ephesians 3:15-21; Philippians 1:2-11; Colossians 1:9-11; 2 Thessalonians 1:2-3; Philemon 4-6.

Thanksgiving Paul always gives enthusiastic thanks for people even if they are criticizing him or sorely in need of correction. Take a note of what he gives thanks for. How would you feel if somebody thanked God for you or your church in those ways?

The scale of asking is in proportion to God's dreams for us.

Make a chart of all the things Paul asks God for in these extracts. Use some of these to pray for your pastor and church leaders, for the young of your church, and other groups.

This may make you feel weak in the knees, but remember that God wants to melt our stony hearts and enlarge our openness.

GROUP IDEAS

Praying the 'Jesus Prayer'

Lord Jesus Christ, Son of God, have mercy upon me / us.

This ancient prayer comes from the tradition of the Orthodox Church. In it I acknowledge that I am a sinner and that I identify with a sinful and suffering society which needs the mercy and healing love of God, freely available in Jesus Christ.

Prayed personally Repeat the prayer silently in time with the rhythms of life – breathing, walking, cycling or swimming. It can be prayed ceaselessly, beginning from a conscious act of the will and descending like an underground stream into the heart, even when the mind is occupied with other things. Thus prayed, it becomes a Christ-centred background to life.

Inevitably it develops as an intercession, as we hold before God a person or an area of strife or sorrow, offering them up to God's transforming grace.

Prayed corporately The prayer can be especially helpful is situations which defy words and seem beyond hope. It is probably advisable to work this in pairs or triplets. Practise the discipline of staying with this prayer alone, allowing it to move around from one person to another, freely and quietly.

Beginners may start with a ten-minute period, but the time can be built up to as much as an hour or two. It will certainly arouse a depth of communion, of joy and pain and insight, once the self-consciousness has lifted, and a rhythm found.

GROUP IDEAS

Praying for forty days

In the Bible forty days is a significant period. It was the duration of the flood (Genesis 7:17); of Goliath's defiance (1 Samuel 17:16); of Elijah's flight (1 Kings 19:8); of Nineveh's fast (Jonah 3:4-5) and of Jesus' testing (Matthew 4). This period always gave way to deliverance from evil and to new beginnings.

Today many are being led to pray for forty days, for specific people or topics – for example, for a family member or a neighbourhood prayer-walk. Does this echo with a particular desire in you, your group, your church? Without desire and the Spirit's help, you won't persevere. Forty days is a long time!

GROUP IDEAS

Pray for the suffering church

Millions of Christians around the world are suffering for the name of Christ. The writer of Hebrews urges us to 'Remember those who are suffering, as though you were suffering as they are' (Hebrews 13:3).

Be as informed as possible. *Open Doors* (PO Box 6, Witney, Oxon OX8 7SP) offers a wide spectrum of information about the world-wide church.

Focus on a single country, or on a few people. If given a chance children have a rich contribution to make in this area of intercession.

Sacrifice, prayer and worship

> This study follows the theme of sacrifice, prayer and worship. The vision of the slain Lamb – the crucified and risen Christ – is the basis and focus for a group session of praise and prayer.

1. *The Lamb who was slain has begun to reign*
Jewish and Christian traditions are blended closely in this passage. A brief look back at Leviticus 9:22-24 or 2 Chronicles 7:1-3 reminds us that the altar was the meeting place between God and his people. In this chapter, God is seated on the throne and before him is the sacrificed Lamb, once slain but now alive. His horns and eyes symbolize power and knowledge.

Reflect on John 1:29 beside Revelation 5:5-6.

2. *The incense of prayer*
Incense was always burnt with the sacrifice. Here it is mingled with the prayers of all God's people, including *yours* (Revelation 5:8). They are being offered to the Father through the Son, the Lamb. In Revelation 8, these prayers are answered by final judgement which brings in God's Kingdom.

Focus this scene in your imagination. Ask the Holy Spirit what prayers to pray into the incense bowls (Revelation 5:8). Spend some minutes listening together in silence. Pray according to the idea in mind, without adding to it.

Revelation 5:5-14 see also Revelation 8:3-5

3. *The Sacrifice of Praise*
Read again the 'new song' in Revelation 5:9-14.

Make these words of praise your own act of worship. Take more time to praise God in words and song.

4. *Offer yourselves as living sacrifices*
It is your turn now to sacrifice yourself for him who has sacrificed himself for you. This may mean a change of behaviour or attitude, or an action linked with your prayers. It is a *free choice*. Keep it *small* – grand gestures are not expected.

Spend a few minutes quietly discerning what you want to offer. Ask the Spirit to help you 'follow the Lamb wherever he goes' (Revelation 14:4). Let the group rest in God before moving back into daily routine.

BOOKLIST

CPAS code	Title	Author and Publisher
03401	**Women at Prayer**	Rachel Stone, Marshall Pickering
03567	**Sister Images**	Mary Zimmer, Abingdon
03550	**You Can Pray**	David Winter, Lion
03565	**Bible Praying**	Michael Perry, Fount
03468	**...and all the children said Amen**	Ian Knox, Scripture Union
03403	**Essentials**	Anne Wright, CPAS

These resources are available from CPAS Sales.

Other Relevant Resources

The Edge of Glory	David Adam, Triangle
Restoring the Woven Cord: Strands of Celtic Christianity for the Church Today	Michael Mitton, Darton, Longman and Todd
What is Celtic Christianity?	Elizabeth Culling, Grove
Restoring the Woven Cord: strands of Celtic Christianity for the church today	Michael Mitton, Darton, Longman and Todd
Songs and Prayers from Taizé	The Taizé Community, Jacques Berthier, Cassell
The Taizé Experience	Brother Roger, Cassell
Life from Within	Brother Roger, Cassell
His Love is a Fire	Brother Roger, Cassell
The Return of the Prodigal Son	Henri J M Nouwen, Darton, Longman and Todd
God of Surprises	Gerard W Hughes, Darton, Longman and Todd
Celebration of Discipline	Richard Foster, Hodder and Stoughton
Silence	David Runcorn, Grove Books
A Kingdom of Priests	Mark Stibbe, Darton, Longman and Todd
Patterns not Padlocks: for parents and all busy people	Angela Ashwin, Eagle
Open to God	Joyce Huggett, Hodder and Stoughton
Keeping a Spiritual Journal	Edward England, Highland
The Practice of Biblical Meditation	Campbell McAlpiine, Marshall Pickering
The *Exploring Prayer* Series	Joyce Huggett (Editor), Eagle
Prayer: finding the heart's true home	Richard Foster, Hodder and Stoughton
Rees Howells: Intercessor	Norman Grubb, Lutterworth Press
Closer to God: practical help on your spiritual journey	Ian Bunting, Scripture Union
Saints at Prayer: a course on praying effectively in groups	Michael Mitton, Anglican Renewal Ministries / Lynx

CPAS, Athena Drive, Tachbrook Park, WARWICK CV34 6NG
Telephone: (01926) 334242. Orderline: (01926) 335855.